PHOTOGRAPHY CREDITS: (c) ©Radius Images/Corbis; 2 (tr) ©imagewerks RF/Getty Images; 2 (br) Mina Doroudi Photography/Getty Images; 2 (bl) ©Alamy Images; 2 (tl) ©DK Dixon/Fotolia; 3 (c) ©Fuse/Getty Images; 4 (c) ©Radius Images/Corbis; 5 (l) ©Uwe Krejci/Photodisc/Getty Images; 5 (r) ©Leonard Lessin/Photo Researchers/Getty Images; 6 (bg) ©Ambre Haller/Flickr/Getty Images; 6 (inset) ©James Randklev/Getty Images; 7 (l) ©David Nunuk/Science Source/Photo Researchers, Inc.

Printed in U.S.A.

ISBN: 978-0-544-07204-6

3 4 5 6 7 8 9 10 1083 21 20 19 18 17 16 15 14
4500470117   A B C D E F G

Sun, Storm, Sun Again

by Kristen Kunkel

HOUGHTON MIFFLIN HARCOURT

spring

summer

winter

fall

The seasons follow the same pattern each year.

Fall comes after summer.

Fall may be cooler than summer.

The weather often changes with the seasons.

warm, sunny morning

Weather can change even in the same day.

Morning Weather

hot, sunny at noon

thermometer

Thermometers measure temperature.
The air can be hot at noon.

storm clouds

rainy afternoon

windy

windsock

A thunderstorm is coming.
A windsock shows it is windy.

warm, clear night

The thunderstorm ends.
The sky is clear again.

Observe and Describe the Weather

Observe and record the weather for one week. Then write a poem to describe how the weather changed from day to day and, if possible, within one day.

Write About the Seasons

Fold a piece of paper in half widthwise. Then fold it in half again lengthwise. You now have a four-page book. Label each page with the name of a season. Write the seasons in the correct pattern. Then write a sentence and draw a picture to show the weather for each season.

Vocabulary

fall	temperature
rainy	thermometer
seasons	weather
spring	windsock
summer	windy
sunny	winter